words
from a man of
no words

OSHO

OSHO MEDIA INTERNATIONAL
New York – Zurich – Mumbai
an imprint of
OSHO INTERNATIONAL
www.osho.com/oshointernational

Distributed by Publishers Group Worldwide
www.pgw.com

Library of Congress Catalog-In-Publication Data is available

Printed in India by Manipal Technologies Limited, Karnataka

ISBN: 978-1-938755-97-2
This title is also available in eBook format ISBN: 978-0-88050-611-3

Every crowd is a motley crowd, but no individual is motley. Every individual is an authentic consciousness. The moment he becomes part of the crowd, he loses his consciousness. Then he is dominated by the collective, mechanical mind. I am doing a simple thing – bringing out individuals from the motley crowds, giving them their individuality and dignity.

I don't want any crowds in the world. Whether they have gathered in the name of religion, or in the name of nationality, or in the name of race, it does not matter. The crowd as such is ugly, and the crowd has committed the greatest crimes in the world because the crowd has no consciousness. It is a collective unconsciousness.

Consciousness makes one an individual – a solitary pine tree dancing in the wind, a solitary sunlit mountain peak in its utter glory and beauty, a solitary lion and his tremendously beautiful roar that goes on echoing for miles in the valleys.

The crowd is always of sheep; and all the efforts of the past have been to convert every individual into a cog in the wheel, into a dead part of a dead crowd. The more unconscious he is and the more his behavior is dominated by the collectivity, the less dangerous he is. In fact, he becomes almost harmless. He cannot destroy even his own slavery.

On the contrary, he starts glorifying his own slavery – his religion, his nation, his race, his color. These are his slaveries, but he starts glorifying them. As an individual he belongs to no crowd. Every child is born as an individual, but rarely does a man die as an individual.

My work is to help you meet your death with the same innocence, with the same integrity, with the same individuality as you have met your birth. Between your birth and your death, your dance should remain a conscious solitary reaching to the stars: alone, uncompromising, a rebellious spirit. Unless you have a rebellious spirit, you don't have a spirit at all. There is no other kind of spirit available.

Osho
The Rebel

When mind knows, we call it knowledge.
When heart knows, we call it love.
And when being knows, we call it meditation.

The authentic question is, "Who am I?" And the only way to know is to be silent, be alert, be aware – watch your thoughts and let them disappear. One day you will find all has become silent, not even a murmur of thought. Everything has stopped, as if time has stopped. And suddenly you are awake from a long, long dream, from a nightmare.

There is only one door which can help you, and that is within you. Taking a jump into yourself, you have plunged into existence. In that moment you feel a tremendous oneness with all.

Then you are no longer lonely, no longer alone because there is nobody who *is*, other than you. There is only you expanded in all directions, in all possible manifestations. It is you flowering in the tree; it is you moving in a white cloud. It is you in the ocean, in the river. It is you in the animals, in the people.

I am not giving you a new set of dogmas, beliefs, creeds, ideologies – not at all. My function is totally different: my function is to take away whatever you have, and not to give you anything in its place because if I take one stone and put another stone in its place, I am even more dangerous than the man who had put the first stone. The first stone was getting old and you were getting tired of it, and it was not giving you any nourishment. It was a stone; what nourishment can it give to you? You were carrying the burden, and slowly you may have become aware that it is better to throw away this stone.

But with a new stone a new honeymoon starts. You start thinking perhaps this stone is the right one. I am not substituting another belief system in you; I am simply destructive. You will be surprised that I am simply destructive – I want to destroy all that has been forced upon you. There is no need to substitute it with anything.

Creativity is your intrinsic potential; I don't have to create it. Once hindrances are removed, you will start growing and flowing, you will start searching on your own. And soon you will gain strength and a new power because even a small discovery on your own will give you such immense happiness that you cannot conceive it. Just a small discovery on your own, and you are a different being because now truth is born in you. It may be just a seed, but the beginning has begun.

Just count how many thoughts are your own, and you will be surprised that not a single thought is your own. All are from other sources, all are borrowed – either dumped by others on you, or foolishly dumped by yourself upon yourself. But nothing is yours.

Remember one criterion: anything precious is only that which you know. And there is no way to lose that which you know. Anything that can be lost, and which you have to cling to, cannot be precious because it can be lost. That shows that it is not your experience.

3

People say that I am brainwashing people. No, I am not brainwashing people. But I am certainly washing their brains – and I believe in dry cleaning!

Start fresh: a clean slate with no belief, with no dogma, with no faith. Then there is a possibility that you may find what the truth is. And the truth is neither Hindu, nor Mohammedan, nor Christian; and the truth is not in the Bible, nor in the Koran, nor in the Gita.

The truth that you will find – you will be surprised – is written nowhere, cannot be written. It is impossible to write it. It has never been uttered by anybody and it is not going to be uttered by anybody.

Your mind is always asking "Why?" and "For what?" And anything that has no answer to the question "For what?" slowly, slowly becomes of no value to you. That's how love has become valueless. What point is there in love? Where is it going to lead you? What will you achieve through it? Will you attain to some utopia, some paradise? Of course, love has no point in that way. It is pointless.

What is the point of beauty? You see a sunset;

you are stunned, it is so beautiful. But any idiot can ask the question, "What is the meaning of it?" and you will be without any answer. And if there is no meaning, then why are you unnecessarily bragging about beauty?

A beautiful flower, or a beautiful painting, or beautiful music, beautiful poetry doesn't have any point. They are not arguments to prove something, neither are they means to achieve any end. Living consists only of those things which are pointless.

Let me repeat it: living consists only of those things which have no point at all, which have no meaning at all – *meaning* in the sense that they don't have any goal, that they don't lead you anywhere, that you don't get anything out of them. In other words, living is significant in itself.

I am not promising you any kingdom of God; you are not going to inherit anything. You have already inherited it.

It is your life. Be loving and respectful to it.

There are miracles that go on happening all around the world; people who have never lived, die – such an impossibility! But it happens every day.

And many have recognized it at the moment of death, and have said it is so: "It is strange; for the first time I am realizing that I missed life."

If you live, for what? – to love, to enjoy, to be ecstatic. Otherwise why live at all?

Respect life, revere life. There is nothing more holy than life, nothing more divine than life.

Existence as such has no meaning. Neither is it meaningless. Meaning is simply irrelevant to existence. There is no goal existence is trying to achieve. There is nowhere it is going. It simply is.

Meaning is goal oriented: some purpose, some achievement. Man's mind brings the problem of meaning.

The mind is the root cause of all the questions that arise in you. The mind cannot rest at ease with things as they are. It is the nature of mind.

The pseudo-religions depend upon disciplining the mind. Real religion's first work is to put the mind aside. And it is, in a way, very simple.

Disciplines are very difficult. To train the mind for concentration is very difficult because it goes on revolting, it goes on falling back into its old habits. You pull on it, and it escapes. You bring it again to the subject you were concentrating on and suddenly you find you are thinking of something else, you have forgotten what you are concentrating upon. It is not an easy job.

But to put it aside is a very simple thing – not difficult at all. All that you have to do is to watch. Whatsoever is going on in your mind, don't interfere, don't try to stop it. Do not *do* anything because whatsoever you do will become a discipline.

Do not do anything at all. Just watch.

The strangest thing about the mind is that if you become a watcher it starts disappearing. Just as light disperses darkness, watchfulness disperses the mind – its thoughts, its whole paraphernalia. So meditation is simply watchfulness, awareness – and that *reveals*. It has nothing to do with inventing. It invents nothing; it simply discovers that which is there.

And what is there? You enter and you find infinite emptiness, so tremendously beautiful, so silent, so full of light, so fragrant – you have entered the kingdom of God. In my words, you have entered godliness.

And once you have been in this space, you come out and you are a totally new person, a new man. Now you have your original face. All masks have disappeared. You will live in the same world, but not in the same way. You will be among the same people, but not with the same attitude and the same approach. You will live like a lotus in water: in the water, but absolutely untouched by water. Religion is the discovery of this lotus flower within.

My whole religious approach is to give you back to yourself.

You have been stolen; you have been covered, conditioned in every possible way. All the doors of approach to yourself have been closed. My whole work is just to make doors and windows in you. And if I can withdraw all the walls and leave you just an open sky, you will know what religion is.

Friendship has disappeared from the world, just as love has disappeared. Friendship is possible only when you meet naked, as you are – not as people want you to be, not as you should be, but simply just as you are. When two people open to each other just as they are, friendship grows.

When two people are ready to drop their masks, they have taken a tremendous step toward religiousness. So love, friendship, anything that helps you to drop the mask, is taking you toward religion.

Inquiry is a risk, it is moving into the unknown. One does not know what is going to happen. One leaves everything that one is acquainted with, is comfortable with. One moves into the unknown, not even perfectly certain whether there is anything on the other shore – or even whether there is another shore.

People cling either to theism, or those who are a little stronger – intellectual, the intelligentsia – they cling to atheism. But both are escapes from doubt. And to escape from doubt is to escape from inquiry. What is doubt? – it is only a question mark. It is not your enemy; it is simply a question mark within you which prepares you to inquire. Doubt is your friend.

The first thing is to be oneself, and the second thing is to know who you are. Remain yourself, remain natural; try to become more and more aware of what this life current is that is running in you.

Who is beating in your heart?

Who is behind your breathing?

Self is that which you are born with. Ego is that which you accumulate, ego is your achievement. Self is a gift of existence to you. You have not done anything to earn it, you have not achieved it – hence nobody can take it away from you. That is impossible because it is your nature, your very being.

Doubt! – and not half-heartedly. Doubt with your total intensity so that doubt becomes like a sword in your hand – it will cut all the garbage that has gathered around you. Doubt is to cut the garbage, and meditation is to awaken yourself.

These are two sides of the same coin, because burdened with all the garbage you will not be able to wake up. The garbage will create sleep in you. That's its function: it is meant to keep you asleep.

Misery has always been there. But to be aware of the misery is a new factor and is the beginning of transformation. If you become aware of something, there is a possibility that something can be done to change it.

People have lived in misery, accepting it as part of life, as their destiny. Nobody has questioned it. Nobody has asked why.

There is something of immense importance about truth: unless you find it, it never becomes truth to you. If it is somebody else's truth and you borrow it, in that very borrowing it is no longer true; it has become a lie.

It is always necessary to begin with the negative, with the no. If you want to reach to yes, you will have to say a thousand no's to find one yes in life. Your whole life has been ruined by so many people, and you will have to say no to all those people. And after a thousand no's, perhaps you may find yourself in a state where you can say yes.

Priests are the greatest con men in the world. Other con men are just small criminals. Of what can they cheat you? But the priest, the prophet, the messiah, the avatar, the *tirthankara* – these are the super con men.

They have sold things which nobody has seen, which nobody is ever going to see.

Whatever you are doing, whatever you are thinking, whatever you are deciding, remember one thing: is it coming from you or is somebody else speaking? And you will be surprised to find the real voice. Perhaps it is your mother – you will hear her speak again. Perhaps it is your father; it is not at all difficult to detect. It remains there, recorded in you exactly as it was given to you for the first time: the advice, the order, the discipline, the commandment.

Ego is all that you go on accumulating through education, manners, civilization, culture, schools, colleges, universities. You go on accumulating it. It is your effort, you have made it, and you have made it so big that you have completely forgotten your real self.

Get rid of the voices that are within you, and soon you will be surprised to hear a still, small voice which you have never heard before. You cannot decide whose voice this is: no, it is not your mother's, it is not your father's; it is not the priest's, not your teacher's… Then a sudden recognition comes – it is *your* voice. That's why you are not able to find its identity, to whom it belongs.

It has always been there, but it is a very small still voice. It was suppressed when you were a very small child and the voice was very small. It was just a sprout, and it was covered with all kinds of crap. And now you go on carrying that crap and you have forgotten the plant that is your life; it is still alive, waiting for you to discover it.

Discover your voice! – then follow it with no fear. Wherever it leads, *there* is the goal of your life, *there* is your destiny. It is only there that you will find fulfillment, contentment; it is only there that you will blossom. And in that blossoming, knowing happens.

Once you have heard a truth, it is impossible to forget it. It is one of the qualities of truth that you don't need to remember it.

A lie has to be remembered continually, you may forget. The person habituated to lies needs a better memory than the person habituated to truth because a true person has no need of memory. If you only say the truth, there is no need to remember. But if you are saying a lie, then you have to continually remember because you have said one lie to one person, another lie to another person, something else to somebody else. You have to categorize in your mind and keep track of to whom you have said what. And whenever a question arises about a lie, you have to lie again. So it is a series; the lie does not believe in birth control. Truth is celibate, it has no children at all; in fact it is unmarried.

Truth comes only to the rebellious, and to be a rebel is certainly to live dangerously.

Society teaches: "Choose the convenient, the comfortable; choose the well-trodden path where, since Adam and Eve, your forefathers and their forefathers and their forefathers have been walking. Choose the well-trodden path. That is the proof. So many millions of people have passed on it you cannot go wrong."

But remember one thing: the crowd has never

had the experience of truth. Truth has only happened to individuals.

The day there are no questions and no answers within you, and you are just sitting here empty, you have come home – from ignorance to innocence.

Living dangerously means whenever there are alternatives, beware. Don't choose the convenient, the comfortable, the respectable, the socially acceptable, the honorable. Choose something that rings a bell in your heart. Choose something that you would like to do in spite of any consequences.

The coward thinks of consequences: "If I do this, what will happen? What will be the result?" He is more concerned about the result. The real man never thinks of the consequences. He thinks only of the act, in this moment. He feels, "This is what is appealing to me, and I am going to do it." Then whatever happens is welcome, he will never regret. A real man never regrets, never repents because he has never done anything against himself.

I teach you to be authentic, integrated individuals with immense self-respect.

With personality there is trouble: the personality cannot melt into anything – into love, into meditation, into friendship. The reason is that the personality is a very thin mask given to the individual by the society. And up till now, every society's effort has been to deceive you and everybody, and to focus your attention on the personality as if it is your individuality.

The personality is that which is given by others to you. Individuality is that which you are born with, that which is your self nature. Nobody can give it to you, and nobody can take it away.

Personality can be given and can be taken away. Hence when you become identified with your personality, you start becoming afraid of losing it. So anywhere you see that there is a boundary beyond which you will have to melt, the personality withdraws. It cannot go beyond the limit it knows. It is very thin, an imposed layer. In deep love it will evaporate; in great friendship it will not be found at all. In any kind of communion, the death of the personality is absolute.

You feel identified with the personality: you have been told that you are this by your parents, teachers, neighbors, friends. They have all been molding your personality, giving a shape to it, and they have made something of you which you are not and which you can never be. Hence you are miserable, confined in this personality.

This is your imprisonment, but you are also afraid to come out of it. You don't know that you have anything more than this. It is almost a situation like this: you think your clothes are you, so naturally you are afraid to stand naked. It is not only a question of the fear of dropping the clothes; the fear is that if you drop the clothes there will be nobody — and everybody will see that there is emptiness. You are hollow within and your clothes go on giving you substance. The personality is afraid, and it is very natural that it should be afraid.

You will be amazed: the moment you are unburdened, you can open your wings in the vast existence that has been awaiting and awaiting you.

If there is heart in your words, the emphasis will come on its own. If there is something that has to be expressed by your hands, the hands will take care of it; you need not do anything. If something comes to your eyes, it will come. You are not to bring it, otherwise the whole thing becomes hypocrisy.

Living dangerously means don't put stupid conditions – comfort, convenience, respectability – between you and life. Drop all these things and allow life to happen to you. Go with life without bothering whether you are on the highway or not, without bothering where you are going to end. Only very few people live. Ninety-nine point nine percent of people slowly commit suicide.

Just the last thing to remember, and it is so absolutely essential I should not be forgiven for forgetting it: live watchfully. Whatsoever you are doing: walking, sitting, eating – or if you are not doing anything, just breathing, resting, relaxing in the grass – never forget that you are a watcher.

You will forget it again and again. You will get involved in some thought, some feeling, some emotion, some sentiment – anything will distract you from the watcher. Remember, and run back to your center of watching.

Watching is not a doing. Just as you watch the sunset or the clouds in the sky or the people passing on the street, watch the traffic of thoughts and dreams and nightmares – relevant, irrelevant, consistent, inconsistent: anything that is going on. And it is always rush hour. Simply watch, stand by the side unconcerned.

The ego is just a mistake, just like two plus two is equal to five. Just like that, when you look inward and search for the real self, you come to know that two plus two is four, not five. Nothing has to be dropped, but something has disappeared from you. Something that was continuously pretending to be your self, something that was destroying your whole life, something that was messing up everything is no longer found.

Please remember one thing: others can fetter you, but nobody can redeem you. Only you can redeem yourself, and that is by stopping others from fettering you – from putting heavier and heavier chains on you, making bigger and bigger walls around you.

You are your own messiah, your own salvation.

You have to remember: watching is not an art, a craft. No, it is a knack. All that you have to remember is not to drown in the river that is flowing inside. And how do you drown in it? If you become in any way active, you are drowned.

If you remain inactive, passive, not doing anything – alert: "I am not supposed to do anything; the anger is passing, let it pass. Good-bye." If some thought is going past, good or bad, don't bother. Your simple concern is to watch, not to give it a name, not to condemn, because all those are actions.

It is none of your business. If greed is passing by, let it pass; if anger is passing by, let it pass. Who are you to interfere? Why are you so identified with your mind? Why do you start thinking, "I am greedy, I am angry"? It is only a thought of anger passing by; let it pass, just watch.

Not speaking is not silence. You may not be speaking, you may not be uttering anything, but inside a thousand and one thoughts are running. There is a continuous flow of thoughts, day in, day out.

Wounds are not healed by covering them. Religion is a cure. The word *meditation* and the word *medicine* come from the same root. Medicine is for the body; what medicine is for the body, meditation is for the soul.

Medicine cures the body, meditation cures your being; it is the inner medicine.

Remember: only what you experience is yours. What you know – only that you know.

Believe and you will never find; whatsoever you find will be nothing but the projection of your own belief – it will not be truth. What does truth have to do with your believing?

Doubt, and doubt totally, because doubt is a cleansing process. It takes out all junk from your mind. It makes you innocent again, again the child which has been destroyed by the parents, by the priests, by the politicians, by the pedagogues. You have to discover that child again. You have to start from that point.

To me, it is the greatest miracle to be in harmony with nature, totally in harmony with nature. When it is morning, you are with it; when it is evening, you are with it. When it is pleasure, you are with it; when it is pain, you are with it. You are with it in life, you are with it in death. Not for a single moment do you differ from it on any point.

This total agreement, this absolute agreement, creates the religious man.

The word *religion* has to be understood. The word is significant: it means putting the parts together, so that the parts are no longer parts but become whole. The root meaning of the word *religion* is to put things together in such a way that the part is no longer a part but becomes the whole. Each part becomes the whole, in togetherness. Each part, separate, is dead; joined together, a new quality appears: the quality of the whole. And to bring that quality into your life is the purpose of religion.

It has nothing to do with God or the Devil. But the way religions have functioned in the world has changed its whole quality, its very fabric, instead of making it a science of integration so that man is not many, but one. Ordinarily you are many, a crowd. Religion melts this crowd into one wholeness so that everything in you starts functioning in harmony with everything else within you, and there is no conflict, no division, no fight – nobody higher, nobody lower; you are just one harmonious whole.

The religions around the world have helped humanity to forget even the meaning of the word.

The concept of God in all the old religions comes out of fear; it is a consolation; otherwise there is no validity no evidence, no proof for the existence of God. The people who believe in God are really people who cannot trust in themselves. They need a father figure, a big daddy.

I am not a messiah, I don't give you any hope. And I would like you to remember emphatically that nobody else can redeem you – the whole idea is wrong. *You* have created your bondage; how can *I* make you free? Throw off your bondage and be free.

You love your chains and you want me to redeem you. You are asking an absurdity. You are the cause of your miseries, sufferings, and you want me to redeem you from your sufferings and miseries. And you will go on sowing the same seeds, continuing being the same old person, watering the same causes. Who can redeem you? And why should anybody redeem you? It is not my responsibility to redeem you. I have not made you what you are; you have made yourself what you are.

We must not leave any nook and corner of existence and our being unknown, in darkness. We have to bring light everywhere. And unless that happens, you will be in misery, you will be in anguish. Your beliefs are not going to help; your faith is not going to help.

When the light is there, the darkness disappears – it is not that darkness escapes. Darkness does not exist at all; it is only an absence of light.

Ego is just like darkness: it has no existence of its own. It is only the absence of awareness. So I don't say drop the ego, I say watch it. Be watchful. Observe it, and you will find it in so many layers that you will be surprised.

Nietzsche says, "Before you can reach to the top of a tree and can understand the flowers blossoming there, you will have to go deep to the roots because the secret lies there. And the deeper the roots go, the higher the tree goes." So the greater your longing for understanding, for cosmic consciousness – because that is the ultimate lotus, the lotus paradise – the further you will have to go to the deepest roots in the darkest underground.

And the way is only one: call it meditation, call it awareness, call it watchfulness. It all comes to the same – first become more alert about your conscious mind, what goes on in your conscious mind. And it is a beautiful experience. It is really hilarious, a great panorama.

In the town of my childhood, there were no movies, talkies. There was no cinema hall. Now there is, but in my childhood there was not. The only thing that was available was that once in a while a wandering man would come with a big box; I don't know what it is called. There is a small window in it. He opens the window, you just put your eyes to it and he goes on moving a handle and a film inside moves. And he goes on telling the story of what is happening.

I have forgotten everything else, but one thing I

cannot forget for a certain reason. The reason, I know, was because it was in all those boxes that came through my village. I had watched every one because the fee was just one paisa. Also the show was not long, just five minutes. In every box there were different films, but one picture was always there: the naked washerwoman of Mumbai. Why did it used to be in every one? – a very fat naked woman, the naked washerwoman of Mumbai. That used to be always there. Perhaps that was a great attraction, or people were fans of that naked washerwoman. And she was really ugly, and why from Mumbai?

If you start looking… Just whenever you have time, just sit silently and look at what is passing in your mind. There is no need to judge, because if you judge, the mind immediately changes its scenes according to you. The mind is very sensitive, touchy. If it feels that you are judging, then it starts showing things that are good. Then it won't show you the naked washerwoman of Mumbai, that picture will be missed out. So don't judge, then that picture is bound to come.

Don't judge, don't make any condemnation, don't make any appreciation. Be indifferent. Just sit silently looking at things, whatsoever is happening.

The mind is very easily able to exaggerate. It enjoys exaggerating, it magnifies things both ways. Just a little pain and it makes so much fuss about it. Just a little suffering and it becomes the greatest suffering in the world. Just a little pleasure and you are on top of the whole world – nobody else knows what pleasure is. You fall in love with a woman and you think, "Never before has such a love happened, and never again is it going to happen. This is unique."

This is happening everywhere, and everybody is thinking: "This is unique!" Mind exaggerates everything, magnifies; it is a magnifier and you believe it.

The mind is part of the society, it is not part of existence. Hence it needs a society for its growth. The better established the society, the more proficiently the mind grows.

Only Bibles, holy books, gather dust. A *Playboy* magazine does not gather dust. Who wants to open a holy book?

Religions have given you comfortable lives, convenient ways of living. But there is no way to live unless you decide to live dangerously, unless you are ready to go into the dark to seek and search for yourself.

And I say to you, you will not find the answer. Nobody has ever found the answer. All answers are lies. Yes, you will find reality; but reality is not the answer to your question. Reality will be the death of your question, and when your question disappears and there is no answer available, that space is mystery.

I do not believe in believing – that has to be understood first. Nobody asks me, "Do you believe in the sun? Do you believe in the moon?" Nobody asks me that question. I have met millions of people, and for thirty years continuously I have answered thousands of questions. Nobody asks me, "Do you believe in the roseflower?" There is no need. You can see: the roseflower is there or it is not there. Only fictions, not facts, have to be believed.

Belief is comfortable, convenient; it dulls. It is a kind of drug: it makes you a zombie. A zombie can be a Christian, Hindu, Mohammedan – but all are zombies, with different labels. And sometimes they get fed up with one label, so they change it: the Hindu becomes a Christian, the Christian becomes a Hindu – a new label, a fresh label, but behind the label the same belief system.

Destroy your beliefs. Certainly it will be uncomfortable, inconvenient, but nothing valuable is ever gained without inconvenience.

You cannot manipulate an integrated man through childish, stupid strategies: "If you do this you will attain to heaven and all its pleasures; if you do that you will fall into hell and you will suffer for eternity." The integrated man will simply laugh at all this nonsense.

He has no fear of the future: you cannot create hell. He has no greed for the future: you cannot create heaven. He needs no protection, nobody to guide him, nobody to take him somewhere. He has no goals, no motivations. Each moment is so complete that it is not waiting to be completed by another moment which will come sometime in this life, or maybe in the next life. Each moment is full, overfull, overflowing, and all that he knows is a tremendous gratitude for this beautiful existence.

That too he does not say, because existence does

not understand language. That gratitude is his very being. So whatsoever he is doing, there is gratitude. If he is not doing anything, just sitting silently, there is gratitude.

You are responsible for whatsoever you are. If you are miserable, you are responsible. Don't throw the responsibility on anybody else, otherwise you will never be free of it. How can *you* be free if *I* am responsible for your misery? Then unless I free you, you cannot be free; it is in my hands. And if it is in my hands, it can be in somebody else's hands.

Those who are with me have to understand, howsoever hard and painful it is, that you and you alone are responsible for everything that is happening to you, has happened to you, will happen to you. Once you accept all your responsibility in its totality, you become mature.

Anybody living according to a rule is destroying himself, poisoning himself, because the rule was found by somebody who was not you, somewhere where you will never be, in some time, in some space, which is not your time and not your space. It is very dangerous to follow that rule. You will be distracting your life away from its center, its grounding – you will misshape yourself. Trying to shape yourself you will only misshape yourself, disfigure yourself.

I never play anybody's game. I play my own game and I make my own rules.

Only blind people believe in light. Those who have eyes don't believe in light; they simply see it. I don't want you to believe in anything, I want you to have eyes. And when you can have eyes, why be satisfied with a belief and remain blind?

You are not blind. Perhaps you are only keeping your eyes closed, perhaps nobody has told you that you can open your eyes.

I am just an ordinary man, just like everybody else. If there is any difference, it is not of quality. It is only of knowing: I know myself, you don't know. As far as our beings are concerned, I belong to the same existence, I breathe the same air. You belong to the same existence, you breathe the same air. You just have not tried to know yourself. The moment you know yourself, there is no difference at all.

It is just as if I am standing and looking at the sunrise and you are standing by my side with closed eyes. The sun is rising for you too, just as it is rising for me. It is so beautiful and so colorful – not only for me, for you too. But what can the sun do? You are standing with closed eyes; that is the only difference. Is it much of a difference? You just have to be shaken and told, "Just open your eyes. It is morning, the night is over."

Just as science discovers in the objective world outside, religion discovers in the inner world. What science is to objective existence, religion is to subjectivity.

Their methods are exactly the same. Science calls it observation, religion calls it awareness. Science calls it experiment, religion calls it experience. Science wants you to go into the experiment without any prejudice in your mind, without any belief. You have to be open, available. You are not going to impose anything on reality. You are just going to be available to the reality whatsoever it is, even if it goes against all your ideas. You have to drop those ideas – but the reality cannot be denied.

The scientific endeavor is risking your mind for reality, putting your mind aside for reality. Reality counts, not what you think about it. Your thinking may be right or may be wrong, but the reality will decide it. Your mind is not going to decide what is right and what is wrong.

The same is the situation of an authentic religion, a scientific religion.

Man is born with an unknown – an unknowable – potentiality. His original face is not available when he comes into the world. He has to find it; it is going to be a discovery, and that's the beauty of it.

That's the difference between a being and a thing. A thing has no potential; it is what it is. A table is a table; a chair is a chair. The chair is not going to become anything else, it has no potentiality; it has only actuality. It is not a seed of something. Man is not a thing. That brings all the trouble and all the joy, all the challenges, all the disturbances.

I am taking God away so that you cannot blame the poor old man. He has been blamed enough for everything: he created the world, he created this, he created that. I take all that blame away from him.

He does not exist. You have created him just to throw your responsibility on him. Take your responsibility back.

The universe wants you to be this way – that's why you are this way. The universe needs you this way; otherwise it would have created somebody else, not you. So according to me, not being yourself is the only irreligious thing.

Be yourself with no conditions, no strings attached. Just be yourself and you are religious because you are healthy, you are whole.

You come into this world absolutely like a plain, unwritten, open book. You have to write your fate; there is nobody else who is writing your fate. Who will write your fate? And how? And for what? You come into the world just an open potentiality, a multidimensional potentiality. You have to write your fate. You have to create your destiny. You have to become yourself.

You are not born with a ready-made self. You are born only as a seed, and you can die also only as a seed. But you can become a flower, can become a tree.

How can you escape from yourself? You can try, but you will always find you are there. You can hide behind trees and mountains, in caves, but whenever you look around you will see you are there. Where can you go from yourself?

When something is very obvious, you start taking it for granted. When something is too close to your eyes, you cannot see it; for seeing, some distance is needed.

So the first thing I would like you to remember is that it is not only today that humanity is miserable. It has always been miserable. Misery has almost become our second nature. We have lived in it for thousands of years. That closeness does not allow us to see it; otherwise it is so obvious.

To see the obvious you need a child's vision, and we are all carrying thousands of years in our eyes.

Our eyes are old; they cannot see afresh. They have already accepted things, and forgotten that those things are the very cause of misery.

It is so cheap to become knowledgeable. Scriptures are there, libraries are there, universities are there – it is so easy to become knowledgeable. And once you become knowledgeable, you are in a very sensitive space because the ego would like to believe that this is your knowledge, not only knowledgeability – that it is your wisdom. The ego would like to change knowledge into wisdom. You will start believing that you know.

You know nothing. You know only books and what is written in the books. Perhaps those books are written by people just like you – ninety-nine percent of books are written by other bookish people. In fact, if you read ten books, your mind becomes so full of rubbish that you would like to pour it out in an eleventh book. What else are you going to do with it? You have to unburden yourself.

Seeing is not thinking. The sun rises: if you think about it you miss it because while you are thinking about it, you are going away from it. In thinking you can move miles away, and thoughts go faster than anything else.

If you are *seeing* the sunrise, then one thing has to be certain: you are not thinking about it. Only then can you see it. Thinking becomes a veil on the eyes. It gives its own color, its own idea to the reality. It does not allow reality to reach you, it imposes itself upon reality. It is a deviation from reality.

Hence no philosopher has ever been able to know the truth. All the philosophers have been thinking about the truth, but thinking about the truth is an impossibility. Either you know it, or you don't. If you know it, there is no need to think about it. If you don't know it, how can you think about it? A philosopher thinking about truth is just like a blind man thinking about light. If you have eyes, you don't think about light, you see it. Seeing is a totally different process; it is a byproduct of meditation.

Simply remain with the life that is dancing in you, breathing in you, alive in you. You have to come closer to yourself to know it. Perhaps you are standing too far away from yourself, your concerns have taken you far away. You have to come back home.

Remember that while you are alive it is so precious – don't miss a single moment.

You can only be yourself, and nothing else. And it is beautiful to be yourself. Anything original has beauty, freshness, fragrance, aliveness. Anything that is imitated is dead, dull, phony, plastic. You can pretend, but whom are you deceiving? Except yourself you are not deceiving anybody. And what is the point of deceiving, what are you going to gain?

Before you can come to know yourself, you have to be yourself. You have to drop all these personalities like clothes, and you have to come to your utter nudity. The beginning starts from there, and then the second thing is very simple.

I can move this hand without any watchfulness, and I can also move this hand while absolutely watching the whole movement from inside. The movements are totally different. The first movement is a robot movement, mechanical. The second movement is a conscious movement. And when you are conscious you feel the hand from within; when you are not conscious you only know the hand from without.

You have known your face only in the mirror, from without, because you are not a watcher. If you start watching, you will feel your face from within. And that is such an experience, to watch yourself from within: slowly, strange things start happening, thoughts disappear, feelings disappear, emotions disappear. And there is a silence surrounding you. You are just like an island in the middle of the ocean of silence, just a watcher — as if a flame of light is at the center of your being, radiating the whole of your being.

Everybody is telling you to keep a low profile. Why? Such a small life, why keep a low profile?
Jump as high as you can.
Dance as madly as you can.

Life is not going somewhere; it is just going for a morning walk. Choose wherever your whole being is flowing, where the wind is blowing. Move on that path as far as it leads, and never expect to find anything.

Hence I have never been surprised because I have never been expecting anything. So there is no question of surprise: everything is a surprise. And there is no question of disappointment. Everything is appointment! If it happens, good; if it does not happen, even better.

It is good to fall a few times, get hurt, stand up again – to go astray a few times. There is no harm. The moment you find you have gone astray, come back. Life has to be learned through trial and error.

Sin is a technique of the pseudo-religions. A true religion has no need of the concept at all. Pseudo-religion cannot live without the concept of sin because sin is the technique of creating guilt in people.

You will have to understand the whole strategy of sin and guilt. Unless you make a person feel guilty, you cannot enslave him psychologically. It is impossible to imprison him in a certain ideology, a certain belief system. But once you have created guilt in his mind, you have taken all that is courageous in him, you have destroyed all that is adventurous in him – you have repressed all possibility of his ever being an individual in his own right. With the idea of guilt, you have almost murdered the human potential in him. He can never be independent. The guilt will force him to be dependent on a messiah, on a religious teaching, on God, on the concepts of heaven and hell, and the whole lot.

To create guilt, all that you need is a very simple thing: start calling mistakes, errors – sins.

Jesus goes on saying, "Repent! Repent!" For what? Because Adam and Eve ate an apple?!

There is only one sin: unawareness. And you are being punished every moment for it – there is no other punishment.

Do you want more? Your suffering, your misery, your anxiety, your anguish – and you are still hoping to be thrown in hell? You are not satisfied with all the misery that you are going through? Do you think hell is going to be better than where you are? What more punishment is there?

Each moment of unawareness carries its own punishment, and each moment of awareness carries its own reward. They are intrinsic parts, you cannot divide them.

Each society goes on propounding: this is right and that is wrong. But can they prevent you from doing what they call wrong? The trouble is, whatever they call wrong is mostly natural – it attracts you. It is wrong, but it is natural, so the deep attraction for the natural is there. They have to create enough fear that it becomes more powerful than the natural attraction. Hence hell has to be invented.

From the very first day the child is born, we start creating a conscience in him: a small part which goes on condemning anything that the society does not want in you, and goes on appreciating anything that the society wants in you. You are no longer whole. The conscience continuously goes on forcing you, so you have to always look out. God is watching! – every act, every thought, God is watching. So beware!

Even in thoughts you are not allowed freedom:

God is watching. What kind of peeping Tom is this God? In every bathroom he is looking through the keyhole; he won't leave you alone – even in your bathroom.

You have to understand these two words: *conscience* and *consciousness*. Consciousness is yours. Conscience is given by the society, it is an imposition on your consciousness.

Different societies impose different ideas on your consciousness, but they all impose something or other. And once something is imposed on your consciousness, you cannot hear your consciousness, it is far away. Between your consciousness and you stands a thick wall of conscience that society has imposed on you from your very childhood. And it works.

Renounce anything and you will become more attached to it than when you had not renounced it. Your mind will move around and around it.

Repression simply means remembering

that your nature is your enemy – you have to fight it, you have to kill it, you have to destroy it, you have to go above it. Only then are you holy.

Now, this is impossible. Nobody has ever been able to go above nature: wherever you are, you are within nature. Yes, you can cripple yourself, you can cut your limbs to the size prescribed by your holy scripture, you can suffer, you can torture yourself as much as you want – but you cannot go beyond nature. Nature is all there is; here is no beyond. Beyond is within nature, not outside it.

So those who are fighting with nature never go beyond it. Their continual failure makes them miserable, makes them mentally unbalanced, psychologically insane. And all these things are good for the priest; he exploits you. His whole profession is to help you, but before he can help you, you must be put in a position where you need the help.

Don't obey anybody; simply obey your being. Wherever it leads you, go fearlessly, in freedom.

Once you see a certain truth you cannot do anything other than obey it. But it has to be your seeing, your perception, your realization. Begin with disobedience.

Society will give you everything if you give your freedom to it. It will give you respectability, it will give you great posts in the hierarchy, in the bureaucracy – but you have to drop one thing: your freedom, your individuality. You have to become a number in the crowd. The crowd hates the person who is not part of it. The crowd becomes very tense seeing a stranger among it because the stranger becomes a question mark.

I say to you: you are responsible only to yourself. And the miracle of this statement is that if you are responsible to your own being, you will find many responsibilities are being fulfilled without being considered at all

Life needs transformation, and transformation is a great work upon oneself. It is not child's play: "Just believe in Jesus Christ, go on reading the Bible again and again, and you are saved." Saved from what? Saved from transformation!

Religion has condemned sex, condemned your

love for food – condemned everything that you can enjoy – condemned music, condemned art, condemned singing, dancing. If you look around the world and collect together all the condemnations from all the religions, you will see that they have condemned the whole of mankind. They have not left a single inch un-condemned.

Each religion has done its bit. If you condemn the whole of mankind completely, a person may simply freak out. You have to do it proportionately so that he becomes condemned, feels guilty, wants to be freed from guilt and is ready to take your help. You should not condemn him so much that he simply escapes from you or jumps into the ocean and finishes himself. That will not be good business.

God is nothing but our idea of the ultimate dictator, the ultimate Adolf Hitler.

I am against prayer because it is basically business. It is bribing God – it is hoping that you can buttress his ego: "You are great, you are compassionate, you can do anything you want." And all this is being said because you want something.

In existence, the smallest blade of grass has the same significance and the same beauty as the greatest star. There is no hierarchy. There is nobody higher, nobody lower.

Existence is very generous: always forgiving, never punishing. But the only way to reach to existence is through your own innermost silence.

To influence means to interfere, to trespass, to drag you onto a path which is not yours, to make you do things which you have never thought of before. To influence a person is the most violent act in the world.

I have never tried to influence anybody. It is another thing if somebody sees some truth in what I am saying or in how I am, but it is not my effort to influence him. If, in spite of me, he is able to see something, then the whole responsibility is his.

Jesus says to his people, "On the judgment day I will sort out my sheep and tell God, 'These are my people – they have to be saved. For others I am not concerned.'" If there is something like a judgment day – there is not, but just for the argument's sake – if there is something like a judgment day, and if I am to do the sorting out, I will not be able to find a single sheep because I have never influenced anybody. And when you influence somebody, certainly you become the shepherd and that person becomes just a sheep. You are reducing human beings to sheep, you are taking their humanity away. In the name of saving them you are destroying them.

Don't be influenced by anybody. Don't be impressed by anybody. Look, see, be aware – and choose. But remember, the responsibility is yours.

Never do any harm to anybody, but never allow anybody to do any harm to you either; only then can we create a human world.

The man who respects himself cannot humiliate anybody else because he knows that the same self is hidden in every being – and even in the trees and the rocks. Perhaps it is fast asleep in the rock, but that doesn't matter; it is the same existence in different forms.

A man who respects himself suddenly finds himself respecting the whole universe.

To feel life and to live life in its totality, and to live it with such passion and intensity that each moment becomes a moment of eternity – that should be the goal of a religion. And that is what I have been teaching to you: eat from the tree of knowledge. Become a knower. All ignorance and darkness should disappear from you. You should become more conscious, more knowing, more aware.

That's what I have been teaching: live life so passionately, so lovingly, so totally, that you can taste something of eternity in it. Whenever you live any moment, forgetting the past, forgetting the future, that moment gives you the taste of eternity.

And Adam and Eve did not commit any major crime – they just had a little curiosity. I think anybody who had any sense would have done the same. It was absolutely certain to happen because there is a deep need in man to know. It is intrinsic, it is not sin.

You have been rewarded with life and consciousness. You are unique in this existence. Trees have life, but not consciousness. Animals

have brains, but not the possibility of awareness.
Man is the supreme-most in this whole existence.

Obedience is the greatest sin. Listen to your
intelligence, and if anything feels right, do it. But
you are not obeying, you are going with your
intelligence.

If your intelligence finds something is wrong,
then whatsoever the risk, and whatsoever the
consequence, go against the order. No order is
higher than your intelligence.

Why have religions put you against your
natural instincts? For the simple reason to make
you feel guilty. Let me repeat this word *guilt*. This
is their focus of destroying you, exploiting you,
molding you, humiliating you, creating disrespect
about yourself. Once guilt is created, once you start
feeling, "I am a guilty person, a sinner," their work
is done. Then who can save you? Then the savior is
needed. But first create the disease.

Once guilt is created in you, you are in the

clutches of the priest. You cannot escape now because he is the only one who can clean all the shameful parts of you, can make you capable of standing before God without being ashamed.

He creates the fiction of God. He creates the fiction of guilt. He creates the fiction that one day you will have to stand before God, so be clean and be pure, and be in such a state that you can stand before him without any fear, and without any shame.

Truth needs no protection. When you speak the truth it is self-evident, complete. Nothing else is needed, no support. It has its authenticity in itself. The lie is empty. It has no evidence. But you can befool people by telling a series of lies. Perhaps one they may find out, but when thousands of lies are told, it is very difficult to find out the basic lie in this crowd.

God is the basic lie – so basic that it needs thousands of theologies in the world to protect it.

It is not a question of believing or not believing – there is no one to believe in or not to believe in. There is no God!

So please remember: don't start saying that I am an unbeliever. I am neither a believer nor an unbeliever. I am simply saying that the whole thing is a mere projection of the human mind and it is time that we stopped this game against ourselves.

It is time that we said good-bye to God forever.

Perfect, absolute, omnipotent, omniscient, omnipresent – these are the words used for God by all the religions; God is dead, cannot be alive, cannot breathe. No, I reject such a God because with such a dead God, this whole universe would be dead.

Godliness is a totally different dimension: then the greenness in the tree, then the flowering of the rose, then the bird in flight – all are part of it. Then God is not separate from the universe. Then he is the very soul of the universe. Then the universe is vibrating, pulsating, breathing: godliness.

When I say God is a fiction, please do not misunderstand me. God is a fiction but godliness is not a fiction; it is a quality.

God as a person is a fiction. There is no God sitting in heaven creating the world. And do you think a God would create such a mess that you call the world? Then what is left for the Devil? If anybody has created this world it must be the Devil, it cannot be God.

You will be surprised when I say that all Christians, deep down, are angry with Jesus. He promised to redeem them, and nothing has been redeemed. He promised, and he was saying, "Soon you will be in the Kingdom of God, soon you will be with me in the Kingdom of God." And two thousand years have passed; that "soon" has not yet been completed. When is it going to be completed?

There is anger in every Christian against Jesus. And because of this anger the Christian shows too much fanaticism for Jesus, so that nobody knows that he is angry. In fact, he himself does not want to know that he is angry, that he has been deceived, that he has been given a bogus belief – that for two thousand years millions of people have lived with this belief and died with this belief, attaining no growth, reaching nowhere, finding nothing. One is afraid of this anger, this rage. To suppress it, he goes to church, he prays to Jesus, or to Krishna, or to Mohammed. But every believer, sooner or later, is going to be frustrated because belief is not going to give him the truth. It is not going to give him the living waters of life.

While Jesus is alive, it is dangerous to be with him. No businessman will come close to him – only gamblers may risk it and be with him. It is dangerous to be with him: he can be crucified, you can be crucified.

But once he is dead it is a great opportunity for business. Then a new kind of person starts gathering around: the priests, the popes, the imams, the rabbis – learned, scholarly, argumentative, dogmatic. They create the dogma, the creed. They create the cult.

On the dead body of a religious person, a cult is created. Christianity is a cult.

What you call religious ideas are not religious, but only superstitions carried down the ages – for so long that just their ancientness has made them appear like truth.

Different methods have been used by different religions to implant the idea that you are born in original sin, but they have to make it certain that you are born in sin. That's why Jesus is born of a virgin girl, because to be born of sex is to be born of sin. Sex is sin.

Now, I again go on wondering how the Holy Ghost made the Virgin Mary pregnant. I don't think he used artificial insemination. In what way did the poor woman become pregnant? But the Christians have to make poor Jesus a bastard, just to keep him away from the sin of sex. Everybody else is born of sex, is born of sin – only Jesus is not: Jesus is special.

You condemn sex, then you become unable to transform its energy. And it is simply energy. It can move in any direction – downward, upward. If you accept it, in the very acceptance it starts moving upward because you are befriending it. The moment you reject it, you are creating an enmity, a division in yourself.

Sexual energy turning downward serves biology, and sexual energy turning upward serves spirituality. But it is the same energy; what name you want to give to it does not matter.

Renunciation is the enforced dropping of

things, and whenever you do anything with force, nothing really drops away. It simply goes deeper into your unconscious. It becomes more of a problem than it was before. Now it will try to come up in different ways, garbs, masks, and you may not even be able to recognize it. But it is going to assert itself, and with force. You have given it that force by forcing it deep down into the unconscious.

When you force something, you are giving force to it. You are making it stronger, and you are making the enemy hide within you, in the darkness, from where you become more vulnerable. When it was in the conscious, it was in the light; you were less vulnerable.

Renunciation is repression.

There is nothing big, nothing great; life consists of very small things. So if you become interested in so-called big things, you will be missing life.

Life consists of sipping a cup of tea, of gossiping with a friend; going for a morning walk, not going anywhere in particular, just for a walk, no goal, no end, you can turn back from any point; cooking food for someone you love, cooking food for yourself because you love your body too; washing your clothes, cleaning the floor, watering the garden...

It is these small things, very small things: saying hello to a stranger, which was not needed at all because there was no question of any business with the stranger. The man who can say hello to a stranger can also say hello to a flower, can also say hello to the tree, can sing a song to the birds.

Ninety percent of the mind diseases in the world are nothing but repressed sexuality, and fifty percent of bodily diseases are repressed sexuality. If we can accept sexuality naturally, ninety percent of your mental diseases will simply disappear, and fifty percent of physical diseases will simply disappear, leaving no trace behind. And for the first time you will find human beings in a totally new age of health, well-being, wholeness.

The golden rule of life is that there are no golden rules. There cannot be; life is so vast, so immense, so strange, mysterious. It cannot be reduced to a rule or a maxim. All maxims fall short, are too small; they cannot contain life and its living energies. Hence the golden rule is significant: there are no golden rules.

An authentic man does not live by rules,

maxims, commandments. That's the way of the pseudo-man. The authentic man simply lives.

Unconscious people are predictable, you can manage them easily. Because they react, you can make them do things, say things – even things that they never wanted to do or never wanted to say.

But a man of awareness, an authentically religious man, only responds. He is not in your hands; you cannot pull him down, you cannot make him do anything. You cannot manage to draw out even a single sentence from him. He will do only that which in that moment he finds, through his awareness, is appropriate.

Without awareness, whatsoever you do you will create more and more problems; they will take you farther and farther away from your nature, and it will be very difficult to solve them, because they are phony.

Even if you succeed in solving them you have not solved anything. Your perversion will start moving in another direction, it will take another shape. It may not come in from the same door; it will find another door. Your house has many doors, of which many are not even known to you.

But with the light, with the flame of awareness inside you, you know your house for the first time, with all its doors and with all its windows. And when the house is lit, then I don't say, "Do this, do not do that." There is no need; you will do only whatsoever is right.

People ask me continually, "What is right, and what is wrong?" My answer is: that which comes out of awareness is right, that which comes out of unawareness is wrong. Actions are not right and wrong. It is the source from where they come which is right or wrong.

Have you ever felt that existence is miserly? What is the need of so many stars? These fools who ask the question – if they meet the creator they believe in – they will ask, "What is the need of so many stars? Why this luxury? A few less won't do? What is the need of so many birds, animals, human beings?"

And do you know that scientists have recognized the fact that life exists on at least fifty thousand planets? We don't know what colors it has taken there – what shape, what beauty, what kind of beings have evolved there – but one thing is certain, that existence is overflowing. With everything it is luxurious. It is not a poor existence, no. Poverty is man's creation.

It is strange that God goes on sitting on his throne, gossiping with the Holy Ghost, playing with his only begotten son, Jesus; and the Devil goes on running the whole world – goes on creating Adolf Hitler, Joseph Stalin, Benito Mussolini, Mao Zedong... The whole of history seems to be ninety-nine point nine percent a creation of the Devil.

Just by saying, "Blessed are the poor because theirs is the Kingdom of God," you don't change poverty. Otherwise, in two thousand years Christian priests would have made poverty disappear. Poverty goes on growing, the blessed people go on growing.

In fact, there will be so many blessed people that in the Kingdom of God, shared by all these blessed people, they will again be poor; they are not going to get much of a share in it.

What is the need of nations? The whole earth is one. Only on maps do you go on drawing lines, and you go on fighting and killing and murdering over those lines. It is such a stupid game.

Unless the whole of humanity is mad, it is impossible to think how it goes on continuing. What is the need of nations? What is the need of passports and visas and boundaries? This whole earth belongs to us, and wherever one wants to be, one has the right to be there.

Politicians and priests have been constantly in conspiracy, working together hand in hand. The politician has the political power; the priest has the religious power. The politician protects the priest, the priest blesses the politician – and the masses are exploited, sucked. Their blood is sucked by both.

Remove God and you remove the politicians, you remove the politics, you remove the priest, you remove the conspiracy between the priest and the politician. And with these two removed, fifty percent of your miseries will disappear.

The world can be really a paradise. In fact, there is no other paradise unless we make one here.

All the religions are teaching, "Serve the poor," but not a single religion is ready to say, "Accept birth control so that the population is reduced."

I am for absolute birth control.

If you respect life, you will start finding it difficult even to pluck a flower. You will enjoy the flower, you will love the flower, you can touch the flower, you can kiss the flower – but plucking it, you are destroying it and you are hurting the plant, which is as alive as you are.

Nonviolence simply says don't kill others. Do you think that is enough? It is only a negative statement: don't kill others, don't harm others. Is that enough?

Reverence for life says share, give your joy, your love, your peace, your bliss. Whatsoever you can share, share. If you are reverent toward life, then it becomes worship, then everywhere you feel existence alive. Then watering a tree becomes worship, then feeding a guest becomes worship.

Any crackpot can push a button and can finish the whole of humanity, the whole of life on the earth. But perhaps deep down, humanity also wants to get rid of itself. Perhaps people are not courageous enough to commit suicide individually, but on a mass scale they are ready.

Religions have given man fictions to live for. Now all those fictions are broken and man has nothing left to live for – hence the anguish. Anguish is not an ordinary state of anxiety. Anxiety is always centered upon a certain problem. You don't have money, there is anxiety; you don't have enough clothes and the cold is coming, you have a certain anxiety. You are sick and you don't have medicine, and there is anxiety. Anxiety is about a certain problem.

Anguish has no problem as such. Just to be seems to be fruitless, futile. Just to breathe seems to be dragging yourself unnecessarily, because what is going to happen tomorrow? Yesterday you were also thinking that something is going to happen tomorrow. Now, this is yesterday's tomorrow, which has come as today, and nothing has happened. And this has been going on for years.

You go on projecting for tomorrow. A moment comes when you start realizing that nothing is going to happen. Then there is the state of anguish. In anguish, only one thing seems to be there: somehow to get out of this circle of life – hence suicide, the increasing rate of suicide and an unconscious desire of humanity that the Third World War happens. "So I am not responsible that I committed suicide. The world war killed everybody, and killed me too."

Always remember: individuals do not commit great crimes. It is always crowds which commit great crimes because in a crowd no individual feels he is responsible for what is happening. He thinks, "I am just being with the people."

Individually, when you commit something, you have to think three times before committing it: What are you doing? Is it right? Does your consciousness permit it? But no, when there is a crowd you can be lost in the crowd; nobody will ever discover that you were also part of it.

What we call democracy has not yet come to the point of being a democracy. Everywhere it is still only a mobocracy because the mass that elects the people is a mob; it is not yet alert or aware.

To me the greatest problem with humanity is that it doesn't know anything of meditation. To me, that is the greatest problem. Neither the population, nor the atom bomb, nor hunger... No, these are not basic problems; they can be easily solved by science.

The only basic problem that science will not be able to solve is that people don't know how to meditate.

Now it has come to a point where either you have to change and throw away all the past inheritance which divides you – and become whole – or you get ready to commit a global suicide. There is only a certain amount of anguish that you can bear. Now it is becoming unbearable. By the end of this century we will be coming to the point when it will become absolutely unbearable. And then there are only two possibilities: suicide or sannyas.

By *sannyas* I simply mean you accept yourself in your totality. You don't bypass any part of yourself, you don't hide anything in darkness. You bring yourself into the light, and see yourself with the eyes of a friend. This is your energy and this is the energy which you have to work upon. When you come to it as a friend, it also comes to you as a friend. And to befriend oneself is one of the greatest things in life that can happen to a man.

Jesus says, "Love your enemies like you love yourself." But he forgets completely that nobody loves himself – how can he love the enemy? And in an even more difficult saying he says, "Love your neighbor as yourself." That is even more difficult. You can love the enemy because he is far away, but the neighbor just banging on your door, how can you love the neighbor? And just like yourself...

I say don't commit that mistake. Because you don't love yourself, if you start doing with your neighbor what you have done with yourself, you will kill him because you have killed yourself. You are living a posthumous existence. Please don't do the same to your neighbor, and never do the same to the enemy. What has he done to you? Why be so ugly to him? It is of course your birthright to do whatsoever you want to do with yourself, but it is not your birthright to do the same with your neighbor or your enemy. No, I would like to say to you that you have never loved yourself. Forget the enemy, forget the neighbor – first love yourself.

Bring your good and bad together, don't divide. Become one, and in your oneness you will see that there is no God outside and no Devil outside. Those were projections of your inner division. Then you will also see outside a wholeness, an immense unity between darkness and light, between death and birth. You will see that unity and wholeness everywhere, hand in hand working together. Nothing is against each other, all are complementaries. What you call good and what you call bad are complementaries. They cannot exist separately, they can only exist together. And to put yourself together is the way to see the universe in its totality, in its togetherness.

I teach selfishness. I want you first to be your own flowering. Yes, it will appear as selfishness; I have no objection to that appearance of selfishness. It is okay with me. But is the rose selfish when it blossoms? Is the lotus selfish when it blossoms? Is the sun selfish when it shines? So why should you be worried about selfishness?

You are born: birth is only an opportunity, just a

beginning, not the end. You have to flower. Don't waste it in any kind of stupid service. Your first and foremost responsibility is to blossom, to become fully conscious, aware, alert; and in that consciousness you will be able to see what you can share, how you can solve problems.

I know one thing for certain, that when you have blossomed you will be sharing. There is no way to avoid it. When the flower opens, there is no way for it to prevent its fragrance and keep it imprisoned. The fragrance escapes. It reaches in all directions. So first be fulfilled, be content. First, be. Then out of your being there will be a fragrance reaching to many. And it will not be a service, it will be a sheer joyous sharing. And there is nothing more joyful than sharing your joy.

You only need power to do something harmful; otherwise love is enough, compassion is enough.

There is no need for war; there is no need for poverty. We have enough money, enough resources, but seventy percent of the whole world's resources go toward war. If that seventy percent is prevented from going toward bringing death to humanity, there is no need for anybody to become less rich. The living of all poor people can be raised higher.

Marx's idea, Lenin, Stalin, Mao – their whole philosophy is to bring the richer people down to the level of the poor people. That they call communism, I call stupidity. My idea is to raise every poor person higher and higher and bring him to the level of the richest person. There is no need for poverty. I will also have a classless society, but it will be of rich people.

M an can live a tremendously rich, blissful, ecstatic life. But the first thing is, he has to accept his responsibility. All the religions have been teaching you to shirk your responsibility: throw it onto God. And there is no God. You don't do anything because you think God is going to do everything – and there is no God to do anything. Then what else can you expect? What is happening and has happened and is going to happen is the natural outcome of this idea of a creator.

If man had been told, "This is your existence; you are responsible whatever you are, whatever you do, and whatever happens around you. Be mature.

Don't remain childish…" But this God does not allow you to mature, his "godness" depends on your immaturity, on your childishness. The more stupid you are, the more gullible you are, the greater is God. The more intelligent you are, the lesser is God. If you are really intelligent there is no God. Then existence is there, you are there – then you create. But the Creator does not allow you to become the creator.

My whole approach is that you are to become the creator. You have to release your creative energies. And this is possible only if this God, who is nothing but a Godot, is removed, absolutely removed from your vision of life. Yes, in the beginning you will feel very empty because that place in you was filled by God. For millions of years he was there; the sacred shrine in your heart was filled with the idea of God. Now, suddenly throwing it out, you will feel empty, afraid, lost. But it is good to feel empty, it is good to feel afraid, it is good to be lost, because this is the reality. And what you were feeling before was only fiction. Fictions cannot help much. They may give you some consolation, but consolation is not a good thing.

What is needed is transformation, not consolation. What is needed is treatment of all the diseases that you have been carrying, not consolation.

The truth is a revelation. It is already there.
You don't have to invent it, you have to
discover it.

Journalists go on searching for sensation – their
whole business depends on sensation. They exploit
the lowest instincts of humanity. Journalism has not
yet come of age, it has not yet become mature. So if
there is a rape it is news, if there is murder it is
news, if there is suicide it is news. Anything ugly,
disgusting, criminal, is news,
and anything beautiful is not news. If a dog bites
a man it is not news, it is natural; but if a man
bites a dog, then it is news. And the journalist is
not interested whether it is true or not; then it
is enough, rumor is enough.

There is an old definition of a philosopher: a
philosopher is a blind man in a dark house with no
light, on a dark night, looking for a black cat which
is not there. This is an old definition of a
philosopher. Let me add something more to it: the
journalist is the man who finds it. Then it is news.

I am continually giving you the right answer to
the wrong question, but nothing else can be done. I

can understand you can't ask the right question. And I can't give you a wrong answer – so what to do? This way it goes on. You go on asking the wrong question, but I don't care much about your question. I go on answering what I want to answer; your question is just an excuse.

You are a harmonious whole. Everything is integrated with everything else. You cannot make one part rich and another part poor. The whole becomes affected, becomes either poor or rich. You have to accept your wholeness. So live, and live intensely. Burn the torch of your life from both ends together. Only such a man can die blissfully, smiling…

A master was dying; it was just the last moment. His disciples had gathered. One disciple asked, "Master, you are leaving us. What is your last message?"

The master smiled, opened his eyes, and said, "Do you hear the squirrel running on the roof?" Then he closed his eyes, died. The disciples were at a loss – what kind of message is this? "Do you hear the squirrel running on the roof?" But that was his whole life's message: just the moment.

At that moment he was enjoying the squirrel. Who bothers about death? And who bothers about the last message? He was in the moment, herenow. And that was his message: don't move anywhere else, just remain here and now. Even at the moment of death – the sound of the squirrel on the roof, and he enjoyed it.

Now, such a man must have lived immeasurably, immensely, incredibly. No regret, sheer gratitude – even smiled. What else do you want as a last message? A smile is enough. And to smile at the door of death is possible only if there are no unlived moments standing in a row behind you, pulling, asking you: "What about me?" – those incomplete moments.

But if there is nothing incomplete – every moment has been completed – there is nothing; it is just silence. And if every moment is completed, there is nothing in the future either, because it is only the incomplete moment which asks for tomorrow. If you have not been able to fulfill it yesterday, fulfill it tomorrow. But if there is no yesterday incomplete, then there is no projection for tomorrow. Then this moment is all.

I have lived without thinking of the past, without thinking of the future, and I have found that this is the only way to live. Otherwise you only pretend to live, you don't live. You hope to live, but you don't live. You remember that you lived, but you have not lived.

Either it is memory or it is imagination, but it is never reality.

Existence knows only one tense: the present tense. It is language which creates three tenses, and creates three thousand tensions in your mind. The present knows only one tense, and that is present. And it is not a tension at all, it is utterly relaxing. When you are totally here, no yesterdays pulling you back and no tomorrows pulling you somewhere else, you are relaxed.

To me, to be in the moment is meditation – to be utterly in the moment. And then it is so beautiful, so fragrant, so fresh. It never gets old, it never goes anywhere.

Man's greatest need is to be needed; otherwise he feels shaken. The trees, the clouds, the sun, the moon, the stars, the mountains – none of them seem to be concerned with you. The whole of existence seems to be indifferent. Whether you are or not, nobody cares. This condition makes the mind very shaky. Then religion comes in, the so-called religion.

The real religion will try in every way to help you drop this need so that you see there is no need for anybody to need you. Asking for it, you are asking for a fiction.

There are things in which a person should be left alone; only then can he discover. If you try to help him you are crippling him.

Don't try to force anybody to take your help while he can manage on his own. Don't force anybody to see through your eyes when he has eyes. And at least, please, don't place your specs on anybody's eyes; your numbers are different. You will drive that person blind, you will distort his vision.

The religious man has no obsession. His life is simple, natural, spontaneous, moment to moment. He has no great ideas that he wants to bring to the world. He has no great ideologies that he wants to impose on humanity.

In deep silence there is no mine and no thine. Life is simply life; it is one flow. We are joined together by invisible threads. If I hurt you, I hurt myself. If I hurt myself, I am hurting you all.

Life is a flux, a movement, a continuum. There is nothing wrong in it. Enjoy that moment which comes and goes. Drink out of it as much as you can because it is fleeting.

Don't waste time thinking. Don't start thinking that it is fleeting. Don't be bothered about what will happen tomorrow, whether this will be with you or not; and don't think of yesterdays. While it lasts, squeeze the whole juice out of it, drink of it completely. Then who cares whether it goes away or if it remains? If it remains we will be drinking it. If it goes, good, we will be drinking some other moment.

It is only the unlived past which becomes your psychological burden. Let me repeat: the unlived past – those moments which you could have lived, but you have not lived; those love affairs which could have flowered, but you missed; those songs which you could have sung, but you remained stuck in some stupid thing and missed the song. It is the unlived past which becomes your psychological burden, and it goes on becoming heavier every day.

That's why an old man becomes so irritable. It is not his fault. He does not know why he is so irritable, why each and every thing irritates him, why he is constantly angry, why he cannot allow anybody to be happy – why he cannot see children dancing, singing, jumping, rejoicing, why he wants everybody to be quiet. What has happened to him?

It is a simple psychological phenomenon: his whole unlived life. When the child started dancing, his inner child was somehow prevented from dancing – perhaps by his parents, his elders, perhaps by himself because it wasn't respected, honored. He was brought before the neighbors and introduced: "Look at this child, how quiet, calm, silent; no disturbance, no mischief." The child's ego was fulfilled. Anyway, he missed. Now he cannot bear it, he cannot tolerate this child. In fact it is his unlived childhood that starts hurting. It has left a wound. And how many wounds are you carrying? Thousands of wounds are in line because how much have you left unlived?

When you are meeting a friend – meet. Who

knows, you may not be meeting again. Then you will repent; then that unfulfilled past will haunt you – you wanted to say something and you could not say it. There are people who want to say "I love you" to somebody, and they wait for years and do not say it. And the person one day may die, and then they will cry and weep and they will say, "I wanted to say 'I love you' to them, but I could not even say that."

I teach you to live tremendously, ecstatically, in every possible way. On the physical level, on the mental level, on the spiritual level – live to the uttermost of your possibility. Squeeze from each single moment all the pleasures, all the happinesses possible so that you don't repent later on: "That moment passed and I missed."

Only very few people live. Ninety-nine point nine percent of people slowly commit suicide.

Out of one seed there can come millions of seeds. Do you see the abundance and richness of existence? One seed can make the whole earth green – the whole universe green, what to say of the earth? Just one seed: so much potential is carried in a single small seed. But you can keep it in your safe, bank account, and live a life which is not life at all.

Whatever you dream, make a note of it: that dream indicates what you are missing in reality. A man who lives in reality, his dreams start disappearing. There is nothing for him to dream. By the time he goes to sleep, he is finished with the work of the day. He is finished, he has no hangover that moves into dreams.

Yesterday cannot be lived. Yes, in the imagination, but not truly. It is dead. There is no way to make it alive again. You cannot move backward in time; that which is gone is gone forever. But millions of people, ninety-nine point nine percent of people, have chosen to live either in the yesterday or in the tomorrow, and the tomorrow is not there and is not going to be there ever. It never comes, by its very nature. It is always coming, coming, coming – but it never comes. It is only a hope which is not going to be fulfilled.

There is no life after death, as you know life. And if there is any life, you have to learn to live now, and you have to live it so totally and intensely that if there is any life after death, you will be able to live there too. If there is not, there is no question. That should always be the rational person's approach.

Be intelligent, and then love will give you all the colors of the rainbow, and you will be fulfilled by many people, in many ways, because one woman will touch one aspect of your being, and other aspects will remain hungry, starved. One man may touch one part of your heart, but other parts will remain without growth. If you cling, then one part becomes a monster and all other parts shrink.

Concentrate your whole energy here now. Pour it into this moment, with totality, with as much intensity as you can manage. And in that moment you will feel life. To me that life is equivalent to God. There is no other God than this life.

To be unhappy, reasons are needed; but just to be happy, no reasons are needed. Happiness is enough unto itself. It is such a beautiful experience that what more do you need? Why should you need any cause for it? It is enough in itself; it is a cause unto itself.

If you create a song, if you create music, if you create a garden, you are being religious. Going to church is foolish, but creating a garden is tremendously religious.

If you can rejoice in this life totally, you will not be bothered at all what happens after death because so much will be happening now that you cannot imagine that more is possible.

What I have given to you is not a closed

system, it is an open experiment. Any truth that may come later on can be absorbed by this system without any conflict because I have told you again and again that there are no contradictions in life. All contradictions are complementaries.

So even something contradicting any statement of mine can be absorbed without any fear because this is my position: every contradiction is a complementary. Just as day and night are complementary and life and death are complementary, all contradictions are complementary. So you can absorb even the most contradictory truth that ever comes in the future and it will be part of my system.

You can make cemeteries beautiful – gardens, lawns, flowers, marble graves – but you cannot hide the fact of death. You can see in every country the cemetery is outside the city. It should really be exactly in the middle of the city so everybody passing by comes to be reminded of death again and again. That is the only thing that is certain. Everything else is just probable: may happen, may not happen.

But death is not a probability; death is the only certainty in your whole life. Whatsoever happens, death is going to be there. You cannot escape from it, you cannot go away from it anywhere. Death will meet you wherever you go.

After a certain age – for example, if you accept seventy as the average, or eighty or ninety as the average – a man should be free to ask the medical board, "I want to be freed from my body." He has every right to not want to live anymore because he has lived enough. He has done everything that he wanted to do and now he doesn't want to die of cancer or tuberculosis. He simply wants a relaxed death.

Every hospital should have a special place for people, with a special staff, where people can come, relax, and be helped to die beautifully without any disease, supported by the medical profession.

If I am saying there is no more significant experience in life than death, I am saying it not because I have died and come back to tell you, but because I know that in meditation you move into the same space as death. In meditation you are no longer your physiology, no longer your biology, no longer your chemistry, no longer your psychology; all these are left far away.

You come to your innermost center where there is only pure awareness. That pure awareness will be with you when you die because that cannot be taken away. All those things which can be taken away, we take away with our own hands in meditation.

So meditation is an experience of death in life. And it is so beautiful, so indescribably beautiful that only one thing can be said about death: it must be that experience multiplied by millions. The experience of meditation multiplied by millions is the experience of death.

It is we who come and pass. Existence remains as it is. It is not time that passes, it is we who come and pass. But it is a fallacy to us: rather than seeing that we are passing, we have created a great invention, the clock – time passes.

Just think, if there is no man on the earth will there be any time passing? Things will be all there, the ocean will still be coming to the beach, crashing its waves on the rocks. The sun will rise, the sun will set, but there will be no morning, there will be no evening. There will be no time as such. Time is a mind invention.

Basically time can exist only with yesterdays and tomorrow. The present moment is not part of time.

When you are simply here, just now, there is no time.

Why should you insist that this moment remain permanent? How do you know that better moments are not coming? Just a moment before you would not have thought of this moment, and who knows, when this moment goes, something better may be on the way. In fact, it is on the way because if you have drowned yourself in this moment totally, you have learned something of tremendous importance. You will be using that in the coming moment. Each moment your maturity is growing.

Each moment you are becoming more and more centered, more and more in the moment, more and more aware, more and more alert, more and more capable of living.

Many of my statements will look contradictory to my old statements. Don't be worried. What I am saying now is the right thing, and whatever I say tomorrow will be more right. The last sentence that I will utter on my deathbed will be ultimately right. Before that you cannot decide. I am alive and I am not in any bondage to the past.

Life has its own ways. The moment you start managing everything, you spoil it. Allow life its freedom.

You have to understand one thing which is very fundamental: the world consists of verbs, not of nouns. Nouns are a human invention – necessary, but after all a human invention. But existence consists of verbs, only of verbs – not nouns and pronouns. Look at this: you see a flower, a rose. To call it a flower is not right because it has not stopped flowering, it is still flowering; it is a verb, it is a flow. Calling it a flower, you have made it a noun. You see the river, you call it a river; you have made it a noun. It is rivering. It would be more accurate to existence to say that it is rivering, flowing.

Everything is changing, flowing. The child is becoming a young man, the young man is becoming old, life is turning into death, death is turning into life. Everything is in continuity, continuous change; it is a continuum. There never comes a stop, a full stop. It comes only in language.

In existence there is no full stop.

A man of awareness is unpredictable because he never reacts; you cannot figure out beforehand what he is going to do. And each moment he is new. He may have acted in a certain way in a certain moment. The next moment he may not act in the same way because in the next moment everything has changed. Every moment life is continuously changing. It is a moving river; nothing is static except your unconsciousness and its reactions, which are static.

Love is a changing relationship, it is not stable. Hence marriage came into existence. Marriage is the death of love.

Almost every husband is suspicious of the wife, every wife is suspicious of the husband. The very phenomenon of marriage exists because you cannot trust. Hence you have to bring the law between you; otherwise, love would be enough.

But nobody trusts love, and there is reason not to trust it. A real roseflower flowers, spreads its fragrance and dies. Only a plastic roseflower is not born, never dies. You have to understand: love, to be real, one day arises, blossoms, flowers – but it is nothing eternal. It fades, it disappears, it dies. You cannot trust it. You have to bring law, instead of love, between you.

Law is a plastic thing. That's what marriage is: love become plastic. Now you can rest assured the law will prevail. Love will die sooner than it would have died if there was no marriage, but you will go on pretending that it is there. Hence the suspicion.

True lovers will understand it: there was something tremendously beautiful, it fulfilled them, it transported them to another dimension. But now it is gone; they will be grateful to each other, they will not quarrel. They have given to each other a few moments of eternity. They will remember those moments, but they will not have any grudge – and they will depart as friends, tremendously grateful to each other.

Why be confined to one love? Why force

yourself to be confined to one love? Nature does not intend it to be so. Nature intends you to know love in as many ways as possible because what you can know from one woman, you cannot know from another woman. What you can know and experience from one man, will not be experienced from another man. Each love is unique; there is no competition, there is no quarrel.

My whole work is to demolish – to demolish all the lies that are surrounding you and not replace them by anything else; to leave you utterly naked in your aloneness. To me, only in your aloneness will you be able to know the truth because you are the truth.

Loneliness is where you are missing the other. Aloneness is when you are finding yourself.

In this life everything is momentary. To me, nothing is wrong if it is momentary – in fact, because it is momentary it is so exciting, so ecstatic. Make it permanent, and it will be dead.

I am not against money; I am against the infatuation. The man who is infatuated with money cannot use it. He is really destroying the money, its very purpose. In every language, in all the languages of the world, money's other name is *currency*. That is significant: money needs to be a current, riverlike, flowing, moving fast. The faster it moves, the richer is the society.

If I have a one-hundred-dollar note with me and I simply keep it in my pocket and never use it, then does it make any difference whether I have it or not? I could have kept any piece of paper; that would have served the same purpose.

But if I use this one-hundred-dollar note and it circulates in this room, and everybody who gets it immediately uses it – so it passes through one hundred hands – then it is one hundred dollars multiplied by one hundred. Then that much money is here in this room. The miser is really anti-money. He is destroying its utility because he is stopping it being a currency.

Happiness is always caused by something: you get a Nobel prize, you are happy; you are rewarded, you are happy; you become the champion of something and you are happy. Something causes it, but it depends on others. The Nobel prize will be decided by the Nobel committee. The gold medal will be decided by the gold medal committee, the university. It depends on others.

Bliss is something totally different. It is not dependent on anybody. It is the joy of creating something; whether anybody appreciates it or not is irrelevant. You enjoyed it while you were making it – that's enough, more than enough.

People reach the highest rung of the ladder then become aware that their whole life has been a wastage. They have arrived, but where? They have arrived at the place for which they had been fighting – and it was not a small fight; it was tooth and nail. It destroyed so many people, using so many people as a means, and stepping on their heads.

You have arrived at the last rung of the ladder but what have you gained? You have simply wasted your whole life. Now, even to accept this needs tremendous courage. It is better to go on smiling and go on keeping the illusion: at least others believe that you are great.

In existence the most extraordinary thing is to be ordinary.

Everybody wants to be extraordinary, that is very ordinary. But to be ordinary and just relax in being ordinary, that is superbly extraordinary. If you can accept your ordinariness without any grudge, any grumbling – with joy, because this is how the whole existence is – nobody can destroy your bliss. Nobody can steal it, nobody can take it away. Then wherever you are, you will be in bliss.

Every man is so unique that he cannot be equal to anybody else. That does not mean that he is higher or lower; that simply means everybody is unique. And there is no question of comparison, the comparison does not arise. The rose is perfectly beautiful being a rose, the lotus is perfectly beautiful being a lotus, the grass leaf is perfectly beautiful being a grass leaf.

You cannot walk on a way made by others for you. You have to walk and make your road by walking. It is not that roads are made available to you readymade: you have simply to walk – no. You have to create the road by walking; just as you walk, you create the road. And remember, it is only for you, not for anybody else. It is just like the birds flying in the sky leaving no trace for any other bird to follow. The sky is empty again. Any bird can fly, but he will have to make his own way.

And to be alone is so beautiful. Untrespassed, nobody trampling on you, you are left to be yourself and you leave others to be themselves.

The integrated man is enough unto himself: he is whole. And to me that makes him holy – because he is whole. He is so fulfilled that there is no psychological need for a father figure, a God somewhere in heaven taking care of him. He is so blissful in the moment that you cannot make him afraid of tomorrow. Tomorrow does not exist for the integrated man. Only this moment is all; there are no yesterdays nor tomorrows.

Accept your aloneness. Accept your ignorance. Accept your responsibility, and then see the miracle happening. One day, suddenly you see yourself in a totally new light, as you have never seen yourself before. That day you are really born.

Religion is nothing but a one hundred and eighty degree turn – from the other to yourself.

As you become more aware, more natural, more silent, more at ease with yourself – not fighting, in a deep let-go – you start seeing habits which are meaningless. And it simply becomes impossible to continue to do them. It is not that you stop doing them; just the opposite. One day you simply find: What happened?

A certain habit which used to be with you twenty-four hours a day has not been there for many days; you have not even remembered it.

Enlightenment means you become full of light. Yes, it is lightening, uncaused – not from the outside, but an explosion within. And suddenly there is no problem, no question, no quest. Suddenly you are at home – for the first time at ease, not going anywhere; for the first time in this moment herenow.

Enlightenment is a very simple and ordinary experience.

If I have seen the open sky, something of that open sky will be carried by my eyes. If I have seen the stars, then something of those stars is bound to be reflected in me. I need not claim it.

If you *re-spect*, if you look again and go deep into your existence, you are going to find the place from where you started losing yourself and gaining the ego. That moment will be a moment of illumination because once you have seen what the ego is, the game is finished.

When you are silent, truth does not appear like an object before you. When you are silent, suddenly you recognize you *are* the truth. There is nothing to see. The seer is the seen, the observer is the observed; that duality no longer exists. And there is no question of thinking. There is no doubt, there is no belief; there is no idea.

To be aware of a dream is the death of the dream.

It has happened to me, so there is no impossibility of it happening to you. I am just an ordinary man, just as you are. If it can happen to this ordinary man, then why not to you? Perhaps you will have to move from a little different angle; perhaps you will have to use a little different method. Perhaps you will have to go a little longer, perhaps from your side the mountain is a little arduous, but it happens!

I am trying to remind you that when you are full of blessings inside, all your questions will disappear: not answered, disappear; dissolved, not solved. And being in that state of no questioning, no doubting, no belief – but utterly fulfilled, contented – knowing happens.

Remember: only what you experience is yours. What you know, only that you know.

Let it be very small, don't be worried; seeds *are* very small, but a seed has potentiality. It is not a thing, it is a being who is ready to burst forth – it just needs the opportunity.

Call it meditativeness, awareness – those are just names – but the essential quality is absolute silence, nothing stirring in you, nothing wavering in you. And in that state, godliness is.

Light comes and goes; darkness always is. When there is light you cannot see it. When light is not there you can see it. But it is always there; you cannot cause it.

Light has a cause. You light a fire, you put on wood. When the wood is finished the light will be gone. It is caused, hence it is an effect. But darkness is not caused by anything, it is not an effect. It is uncaused eternity.

Nirvana is a very simple phenomenon. It simply means blowing out the small candle of the ego. And suddenly... The reality has always been there, but just because of the candle of the ego you were not able to see it. Now the candle is no longer there, the reality is. It has always been there. You had never lost it in the first place. One cannot lose it even if one tries. It is your very nature, so how can you lose it? It is you – your very being. Yes, you can forget at the most.

Now, see the emphasis. It is not an achievement. Achievement is in the future, far away. Achievement is difficult, can be almost impossible, will take time, will take will and willpower, struggle. No, it is not an achievement. You have not lost it. Even if you want to lose it, there is no way to lose it. Wherever you go it will go with you. It is you; how can you escape from yourself? You can try, but you will always find you are there. You can hide behind trees and mountains, in caves, but whenever you look around you will see you are there. Where can you go from yourself?

So, nirvana is just like darkness. The light is put out and your reality is all there, with all its beauty, benediction, blessing.

In the beginning there was silence, not sound.
In the middle there is silence.
In the end there is silence.

ABOUT OSHO

Osho's unique contribution to the understanding of who we are defies categorization. Mystic and scientist, a rebellious spirit whose sole interest is to alert humanity to the urgent need to discover a new way of living. To continue as before is to invite threats to our very survival on this unique and beautiful planet.

His essential point is that only by changing ourselves, one individual at a time, can the outcome of all our "selves" – our societies, our cultures, our beliefs, our world – also change. The doorway to that change is meditation.

Osho the scientist has experimented and scrutinized all the approaches of the past and examined their effects on the modern human being and responded to their shortcomings by creating a new starting point for the hyperactive 21st Century mind: OSHO Active Meditations.

Once the agitation of a modern lifetime has started to settle, "activity" can melt into "passivity," a key starting point of real meditation. To support this next step, Osho has transformed the ancient "art of listening" into a subtle contemporary methodology: the OSHO Talks. Here words become music, the listener discovers who is listening, and the awareness moves from what is being heard to the individual doing the listening. Magically, as silence arises, what needs to be heard is understood directly, free from the distraction of a mind that can only interrupt and interfere with this delicate process.

These thousands of talks cover everything from the individual quest for meaning to the most urgent social and political issues facing society today. Osho's books are not written but are transcribed from audio and video recordings of these extemporaneous talks to international audiences. As he puts it, "So remember: whatever I am saying is not just for you...I am talking also for the future generations."

Osho has been described by *The Sunday Times* in London as one of the "1000 Makers of the 20th Century" and by American author Tom Robbins as "the most dangerous man since Jesus Christ." *Sunday Mid-Day* (India) has selected Osho as one of ten people – along with Gandhi, Nehru and Buddha – who have changed the destiny of India.

About his own work Osho has said that he is helping to create the conditions for the birth of a new kind of human being. He often characterizes this new human being as "Zorba the Buddha" – capable both of enjoying the earthy pleasures of a Zorba the Greek and the silent serenity of a Gautama the Buddha.

Running like a thread through all aspects of Osho's talks and meditations is a vision that encompasses both the timeless wisdom of all ages past and the highest potential of today's (and tomorrow's) science and technology.

Osho is known for his revolutionary contribution to the science of inner transformation, with an approach to meditation that acknowledges the accelerated pace of contemporary life. His unique OSHO Active Meditations™ are designed to first release the accumulated stresses of body and mind, so that it is then easier to take an experience of stillness and thought-free relaxation into daily life.

Two autobiographical works by the author are available:
Autobiography of a Spiritually Incorrect Mystic,
St Martins Press, New York (book and eBook)
Glimpses of a Golden Childhood,
OSHO Media International,
Pune, India (book and eBook)

OSHO INTERNATIONAL
MEDITATION RESORT

Each year the Meditation Resort welcomes thousands of people from more than 100 countries. The unique campus provides an opportunity for a direct personal experience of a new way of living – with more awareness, relaxation, celebration and creativity. A great variety of around-the-clock and around-the-year program options are available. Doing nothing and just relaxing is one of them!

All of the programs are based on Osho's vision of "Zorba the Buddha" – a qualitatively new kind of human being who is able *both* to participate creatively in everyday life *and* to relax into silence and meditation.

Location
Located 100 miles southeast of Mumbai in the thriving modern city of Pune, India, the OSHO International Meditation Resort is a holiday destination with a difference. The Meditation Resort is spread over 28 acres of spectacular gardens in a beautiful tree-lined residential area.

OSHO Meditations
A full daily schedule of meditations for every type of

person includes both traditional and revolutionary methods, and particularly the OSHO Active Meditations™. The daily meditation program takes place in what must be the world's largest meditation hall, the OSHO Auditorium.

OSHO Multiversity

Individual sessions, courses and workshops cover everything from creative arts to holistic health, personal transformation, relationship and life transition, transforming meditation into a lifestyle for life and work, esoteric sciences, and the "Zen" approach to sports and recreation. The secret of the OSHO Multiversity's success lies in the fact that all its programs are combined with meditation, supporting the understanding that as human beings we are far more than the sum of our parts.

OSHO Basho Spa

The luxurious Basho Spa provides for leisurely open-air swimming surrounded by trees and tropical green. The uniquely styled, spacious Jacuzzi, the saunas, gym, tennis courts…all these are enhanced by their stunningly beautiful setting.

Cuisine

A variety of different eating areas serve delicious Western, Asian and Indian vegetarian food – most of it organically grown especially for the Meditation

Resort. Breads and cakes are baked in the resort's own bakery.

Night life
There are many evening events to choose from – dancing being at the top of the list! Other activities include full-moon meditations beneath the stars, variety shows, music performances and meditations for daily life.

Facilities
You can buy all of your basic necessities and toiletries in the Galleria. The Multimedia Gallery sells a large range of OSHO media products. There is also a bank, a travel agency and a Cyber Café on-campus. For those who enjoy shopping, Pune provides all the options, ranging from traditional and ethnic Indian products to all of the global brand-name stores.

Accommodation
You can choose to stay in the elegant rooms of the OSHO Guesthouse, or for longer stays on campus you can select one of the OSHO Living-In programs. Additionally there is a plentiful variety of nearby hotels and serviced apartments.

www.osho.com/meditationresort
www.osho.com/guesthouse
www.osho.com/livingin

FOR MORE INFORMATION

www.**OSHO**.com

a comprehensive multi-language website including a magazine, OSHO Books, OSHO Talks in audio and video formats, the OSHO Library text archive in English and Hindi and extensive information about OSHO Meditations. You will also find the program schedule of the OSHO Multiversity and information about the OSHO International Meditation Resort.

http://OSHO.com/AllAboutOSHO
http://OSHO.com/Resort
http://OSHO.com/Shop
http://www.youtube.com/OSHO
http://www.Twitter.com/OSHO
http://www.facebook.com/pages/OSHO.
International

To contact OSHO International Foundation:
www.osho.com/oshointernational,
oshointernational@oshointernational.com